ANIMAL
ARCHITECTS

JOHN NICHOLSON

ALLEN&UNWIN

Acknowledgements

I am grateful to the following organisations and individuals for their help: Sarah Brenan, Liz Fields, Dr Michael Grounds, Greg Hunt, Gisela Kaplan, Melbourne's Open Range Zoo, Museum Victoria, Sandra Nobes, Rory O'Brien, Rosalind Price, Gail Spooner.

First published in 2003

Allen & Unwin
83 Alexander St
Crows Nest NSW 2065
Australia
Phone: (61 2) 8425 0100
Fax: (61 2) 9906 2218
Email: frontdesk@allen-unwin.com.au
Web: http://www.allenandunwin.com

National Library of Australia
Cataloguing-in-Publication entry:

Nicholson, John, 1950– .
  Animal architects.

  Bibliography.
  Includes index.
  For primary school children.
  ISBN 1 86508 955 9.

  1. Animals – Habitations – Juvenile literature. I. Title.

591.564

Designed and typeset by Sandra Nobes
Printed in Singapore by Imago Productions Pty Ltd

10 9 8 7 6 5 4 3 2

◀ **TITLE PAGE** *Martins and swallows build bottle-shaped nests out of tiny lumps of mud*

Contents

What this book is about

This book describes the intricate and beautiful structures that animals create – places to live in safely, raise young and store food.

Some creatures, like termites, seem to build by instinct; others, especially birds, have to learn and practise before they become skilled home-builders. Either way, the results are truly impressive, from the beaver's massive dams and lodges to the nautilus' delicate shell, from termites' air-conditioned skyscrapers to the finely woven warbler's nest with its tiny verandah roof. The animals that build the best shelters have the best chance of surviving and raising their young successfully.

COLLECTOR BIRD *The great bowerbird of northern Australia builds two parallel rows of twigs and grass, arching over at the top and about one metre long. At one end of the bower, the male displays his collection of white and pale yellow objects. He arranges and rearranges them in groups over and over and over again. The satin bowerbird also builds a bower, but collects mainly blue and green objects.*

CHAPTER 1

NOMADS

Many animals carry their homes around with them. Sometimes these homes are in the form of a hard shell attached to the animal, protecting it from predators – like armour. Other animals can move into and out of their shells, or even take over other animals' shells.

A home on its back
green turtle

Green turtles live encased in a suit of armour that grows as they grow. The rigid upper shell or carapace is like a 'jigsaw' of thick, hard bony plates fused (joined) together and covered in a thin layer of keratin (our fingernails are made of keratin, too). The carapace is joined onto the turtle's ribs and backbone. A thinner shell called the plastron protects the turtle's undersides.

Sadly, this armour-plating does not protect turtles from humans. So many have been killed that the green turtle is now a highly endangered species.

Green turtles can be a metre long and weigh as much as 150 kg. They live for up to 100 years.

Beach houses *shellfish, snails*

Soft-bodied creatures called molluscs have been around for at least 500 million years. Snails, limpets and oysters are all molluscs. They have their own mobile homes – hard protective shells that they carry around wherever they go. There is a huge variety of molluscs. They have adapted to a startling range of different habitats, from the tropics to the Arctic regions, from the highest mountains to the deepest oceans, but most of them live in shallow coastal waters.

COLLECTOR'S ITEM *Collectors hunt eagerly for this beautiful shell – the precious wentletrap or staircase shell.*

THE FABLED NAUTILUS
Nautilus shells are divided into many different chambers – up to 36. The mollusc lives in the most newly made and largest chamber. Each of the separating walls has a small opening, and a thin cord of flesh stretches back through these openings to all the previous chambers.

    Between 50 million and 100 million years ago, there were thousands of different species of nautiloids. One of the earliest was a carnivorous monster with a long tapering shell over 5 metres long! It must have been very unwieldy. No wonder nautiluses evolved into today's more compact spiral.

TULIP SHELLS *can be found in both shallow and deep water. Their inhabitants live on worms and other shellfish.*

MUREX SHELLS *live on rocks or coral, or in the sand or mud in shallow coastal waters. People sometimes use them for combs.*

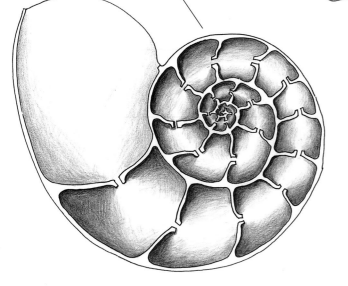

MONEY SHELL *Many people believe that cowries have magical powers. They are often used as good-luck charms. Over 4000 years ago, people started using small cowries as money. They soon became the most widely used currency the world has ever known. For thousands of years cowrie shells could be used to buy things throughout Europe, Russia, Africa, the Middle East, Asia and the Pacific. They were still being used in parts of Africa less than 100 years ago.*

How a shell is made

To build its home the mollusc secretes ('sweats') a watery mixture of calcium carbonate that then hardens around its body to form a shell. As it grows, the mollusc enlarges its shell. This is why many shells consist of a gradually widening tunnel, usually wrapped around itself in a spiral.

If the shell gets damaged, the mollusc can repair it by filling cracks and patching holes with more calcium carbonate.

Some molluscs have a bony disc at the back of their 'foot' (the bit of their body that slides along the ground). The disc forms a hard trapdoor, which covers the opening to the shell when the mollusc stops feeding and pulls itself inside.

People have used shells to make all sorts of useful objects: water containers, trumpets, jewellery, buttons, good-luck charms, knives, bailers, scoops – even money!

WHELKS *can be big or little. They live in both shallow and deep water, feeding on worms, other molluscs and dead fish.*

BEWARE! *The many types of* **cone shell** *have a poisonous bite which can kill humans. If you see one, don't touch it! Some live in the shallows, others in deeper water. They are specialised predators – some eat only other molluscs, some eat worms and others eat fish.*

AUGER SHELLS *The occupants of these shells burrow into the mud or sand in intertidal zones, feeding on worms. They are venomous, but not dangerous to humans.*

GREEN TREE SNAILS *live in trees on Manus Island (near Papua New Guinea). Shell collectors love their beautiful colours – iridescent green with narrow golden bands. So many of these shells have been collected that the species is now in danger of extinction.*

THAIS SHELLS *are related to Murex.*

SCREW SHELL MOLLUSCS *are mud- and sand-dwellers, living just below low tide level. They eat scraps of dead animals.*

SUNDIALS *live in shallow water and feed on coral and sea anemones.*

VIOLET SNAILS *These small fat shellfish float upside down on the ocean's surface, usually in large groups, held up by a mass of air bubbles trapped in mucus.*

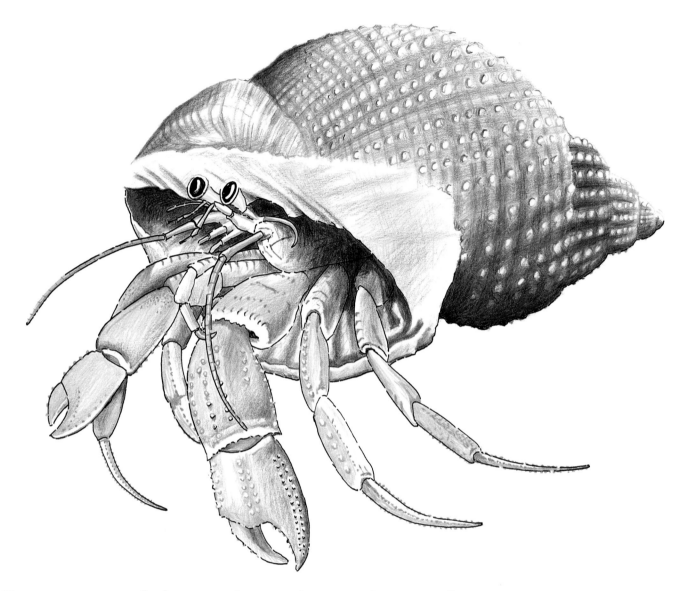

Borrowed housing *hermit crab*

Most crabs grow their own armour-plating and carry it around with them – but not the hermit crab. Over the centuries, this extraordinary creature has become adapted to make use of the millions of discarded mollusc shells that litter the ocean floor. Hermit crabs have evolved a spiral-shaped body that fits neatly into a whelk or similar-shaped shell, and a pair of back legs that can grip onto the inside of its borrowed home.

As the crab outgrows its shell, it goes looking for a larger one. It only leaves the safety of its old shell when it finds what looks like a suitable new one. Even then it will return to the old shell if it finds the new one is a bad fit, too heavy, or awkward to drag around.

Hermit crabs always use empty shells – they never kill a mollusc in order to steal its shell. Sometimes two hermit crabs fight over an empty shell that they both want.

CHAPTER 2

DIGGERS

Under the ground, some animals occupy a maze of tunnels and subterranean chambers. Other animals scrape out simpler holes in the ground in which to sleep or lay their eggs.

A thermometer in its beak *Mallee fowl*

Mallee fowls' desert habitat is scorching hot during the day and freezing at night, but they still manage to keep their eggs at just the right temperature. Here's how they do it.

In April the male Mallee fowl digs a large hole. In it he piles up leaves from 40 metres around. As the leaves start to rot, they warm up like a compost heap.

In August he covers the mound with a thick layer of sandy soil. From now on, he checks the temperature every day – digging a hole in the mound, jumping in and taking a small amount of compost in his heat-sensitive beak, then spitting it out. When he's satisfied, he invites the female to take a look. Sometimes she is hard to please and he has to dig another hole for her. From about mid-September she starts laying eggs in the mound – one every four days until February. That's a lot of eggs!

The male keeps up his daily inspections, changing the mound if the temperature is not right.

On autumn or winter days when the eggs may get too cold, he scratches away a deep crater in the top of the mound, leaving just a thin layer of sand so the sun's rays can heat the leaf pile underneath. The removed sand is spread out in the sun to warm up. The Mallee fowl keeps turning it over, so it heats up as much as possible before he piles it all back on the mound, to keep the compost warm at night. Doing all this takes about five hours! – most of the day.

In summer, when the eggs could get too hot, he is up very early in the morning, scratching a crater in the mound. This lets in cool air. In the middle of the day, he piles as much sand as possible on top, to insulate the eggs from the hot sun.

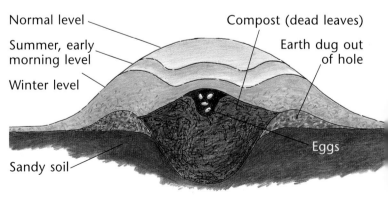

Normal level
Summer, early morning level
Winter level
Compost (dead leaves)
Earth dug out of hole
Eggs
Sandy soil

CROSS-SECTION through a Mallee-fowl mound

Great excavations *wombat*

Wombats are the earth-movers of the animal world. These tough little balls of muscle on stumpy legs shift masses of soil to create large, complex warrens of connected tunnels and sleeping chambers. They prefer the soft soil near a creek, tunnelling into the sloping sides of the gully. An adult wombat uses a number of different burrows, sharing them with other wombats. Burrows sometimes link up with neighbouring burrows, creating even bigger networks of tunnels.

NESTS *The wombat enlarges parts of the warren by lying on its back or side to scrape extra soil out of the roof or walls of a tunnel. This creates oval rooms or nests about one metre long and half a metre wide. Then the wombat brings leaves, bark, grass and bracken fronds to carpet the floor and make a comfortable sleeping place.*

The wombat just bites off any roots that get in the way.

Soil dug from the warren forms a flat mound outside the entrance.

THE BURROW is a network of tunnels *with several entrances. This warren has about 30 metres of tunnel.*

Scoop, shovel and sweep

Back legs firmly braced, the wombat uses its front paws, one at a time, scooping out the soil with its strong claws and sweeping it backwards with flat, spade-like palms. It then uses its back legs to throw the soil further back still. When it has a big enough pile, it backs out of the tunnel, using all four paws to clear the soil away. Wombats work in 20-minute bursts, then rest. In soft soil they can dig about two metres of tunnel in a night.

When they're not 'dozing, they're dozing

Wombats spend about two-thirds of their lives in their burrows – mainly sleeping. In the late afternoon they doze near the entrance, waiting for sunset, when they will come out and feed.

Underground homes *badger, prairie dog, meerkat, rabbit, naked mole rat*

Badgers construct some of the world's grandest and most extensive underground homes. A badgers' 'set' contains a labyrinth of interconnecting tunnels on several levels. It can be 30 metres from one end of a set to the other. About twelve individuals live in each set. Many generations may occupy one set, constantly enlarging and improving it.

In Mexico and the USA, prairie dogs establish enormous colonies made up of lots of individual family groups, each with its own burrow and territory. The entrance to the burrow is a vertical shaft diving as much as 5 metres down into the ground. Two or three horizontal passages lead off from the shaft, ending in rounded nesting chambers, thickly cushioned with grass. The prairie dogs' semi-desert habitat is freezing cold at night, but they stay warm and safe in their burrows because they are so far below ground level.

Prairie dogs pile the soil dug from their burrow into cone-shaped mounds around the entrance. These mounds keep rain and melting snow out of the burrow. They also serve

MEERKATS *(right) are brave and loyal, hard-working, co-operative and affectionate. No wonder people in some parts of Africa keep them as pets.*

They live in extended family groups of between 10 and 30 meerkats, each group occupying hundreds of hectares. Their territory is peppered with nests, burrows and bolt-holes (small 'air-raid' shelters for emergencies). Wherever they are foraging, they always seem to know exactly where the nearest hole is. Like prairie dogs, they have lookouts, keeping watch for predators. The others can feed in peace, but they are ready to bolt at the first warning call, to the nearest burrow or bolt-hole.

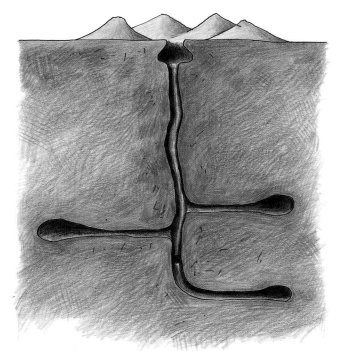

CROSS-SECTION through a prairie dog's home

as lookout points. While the other prairie dogs graze, two or three stand on their hind legs on the mounds, and scan the surroundings for predators. An enlarged area just inside the burrow entrance provides quick temporary safety if danger stalks.

Rabbit burrows also have a vertical shaft. This is not an entrance, but an escape route. When a predator enters the burrow, the rabbit pops out from the shaft like a cork from a champagne bottle.

One of the strangest of underground dwellers, the naked mole rat, is a chunky, hairless, nearly-blind little animal that lives most of its life underground. Naked mole rats live in colonies of 20-30 individuals ruled by a dominant female.

Entry to the underworld
trapdoor spider

The trapdoor spider fits a thick, tight lid to the entrance of its underground home. This is made of sand and pebbles bound together with silk. Silk also forms the hinge, so the trapdoor is easy to push open, but will then drop back automatically into place. The spider lies in wait, two legs sticking out and its trapdoor slightly ajar, for an ant, fly or small beetle to wander by. The outside of the trapdoor is beautifully camouflaged to blend in with the surrounding ground. The door fits so tightly that heavy rain cannot flood the nest.

SILK-LINED *The trapdoor spider coats the inside of its tunnel with a mixture of soil and saliva and then partly covers it with silk.*

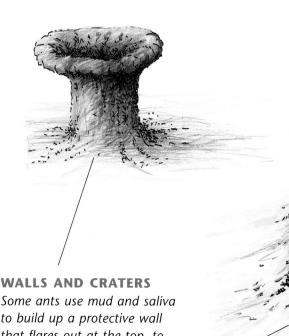

WALLS AND CRATERS
Some ants use mud and saliva to build up a protective wall that flares out at the top, to prevent flooding and to discourage predators. Others build a large crater for the same purpose, using the sand and soil dug out of the nest.

14

CHAPTER 3

W E A V E R S

Some birds build the roughest, untidiest nests imaginable. Others weave elaborate, cosy homes complete with doors, corridors and separate rooms. But for delicacy and intricacy, nothing beats the webs spun by spiders to catch and kill their prey.

Tiny tree huts *gerygone, crested bellbird, rufous fantail*

Snake-proof...

This hanging nest belongs to the brown gerygone (sometimes called brown warbler) that lives in the rainforests of eastern Australia. It is made of materials from the rainforest: twigs, moss, small roots and lichen.

Many bird species have adapted their nests to hang from the branches (instead of perching on top of them) in areas where tree-snakes live. It is more difficult for snakes to discover chicks in a hanging nest, and harder for predator birds to get in.

...and water-proof

The tiny entrance hole has a little verandah roof to keep the rain off.

The crested bellbird lives in Australia's dry inland. It decorates the rim of its nest with hairy caterpillars – probably to frighten off predators. The large, deep nest is built from twigs, bark, grasses, roots and leaves, usually in a fork between two large branches.

Paradise riflebirds have similar decorating ideas – decorating the rims of their nests with cast-off snake-skins!

Rufous fantails – named because of the reddish-brown feathers on their backs and foreheads – build a cup-shaped nest with a 'wine-glass' stem hanging beneath. They live in the rainforests of eastern and far northern Australia. The nest is made of grass and thin twigs at the junction of three or four small branches. They weave the nest around the branches, tying it on firmly so it can't fall off.

A safe and cosy place
titmouse

Not a mouse at all, the titmouse is actually a small bird found in Europe, Africa and North America. Its cosy-looking nest hangs from a couple of spindly twigs at the end of a branch. Most predators are too heavy to crawl out along such a thin branch. Building a small side entrance instead of leaving the nest open at the top also helps to protect the nest from predators.

One African titmouse even has a door! – a flap of woven sticks and grass attached to the bottom of the opening. It can swing up like a drawbridge to cover the entry hole.

Young birds have to practise for a long time to build good nests.

Strongly built and padded with feathers, wool and furry seeds, titmouse nests have often been used by people for other purposes. Masai people in Africa used them as purses. Children in Eastern Europe would try to collect a pair of them. Turn the picture on its side and see if you can work out what they did with them.

Building the nest takes three or four weeks.

STAGE 1 The titmouse starts by winding strands of straw, grass or hair around one or two twigs, leaving the end of each strand hanging down.

STAGE 2 He brings other material and weaves it in with the hanging strands to form a thick matted rope hanging down.

STAGE 3 He extends the rope down, dividing it into two flaps of woven material. He then brings together the two flaps at the bottom, to form a kind of sling.

FINALLY He fills in the openings at both ends of the sling, leaving a small hole near the top of one end.

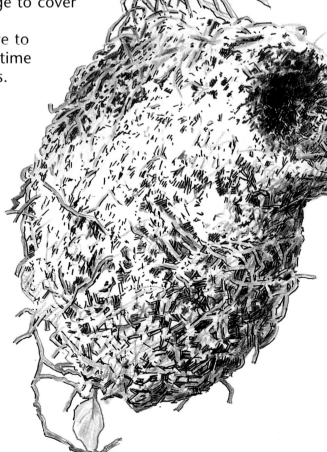

17

Work of a master *weaver bird*

Weaver birds are among the most skilful builders of the animal world. Their complicated nests seem to be made of the finest basketware.

Like other birds, they must practise to get their nests right. Their early efforts are often very rough and clumsy, and if they choose the wrong knot, the weight of grass and bird may bring the whole nest down.

The male bird constructs the nest, making it as good as he can in order to attract a mate. If he is unsuccessful, he will pull it to pieces and start again.

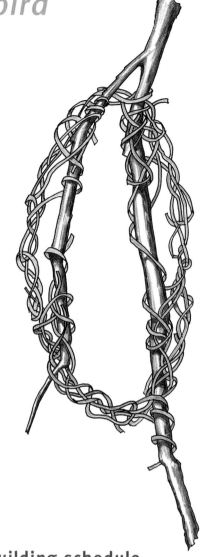

The building schedule

First, he chooses a strong forked twig hanging downwards and uses it to support a circle of woven grass and stalks.

Then he gradually extends the circle outwards, creating a 'half-ball' on one side. This will be the 'brood chamber' for rearing the young. He also extends the circle out the other side, creating another 'room', but leaving a hole in it for the entrance.

Finally he builds a long tube hanging down from the entrance hole. This long 'flight tube' is the only entry to the nest, providing protection against even the most determined tree-snakes.

The female pads out the inside with feathers, grass and other soft stuff.

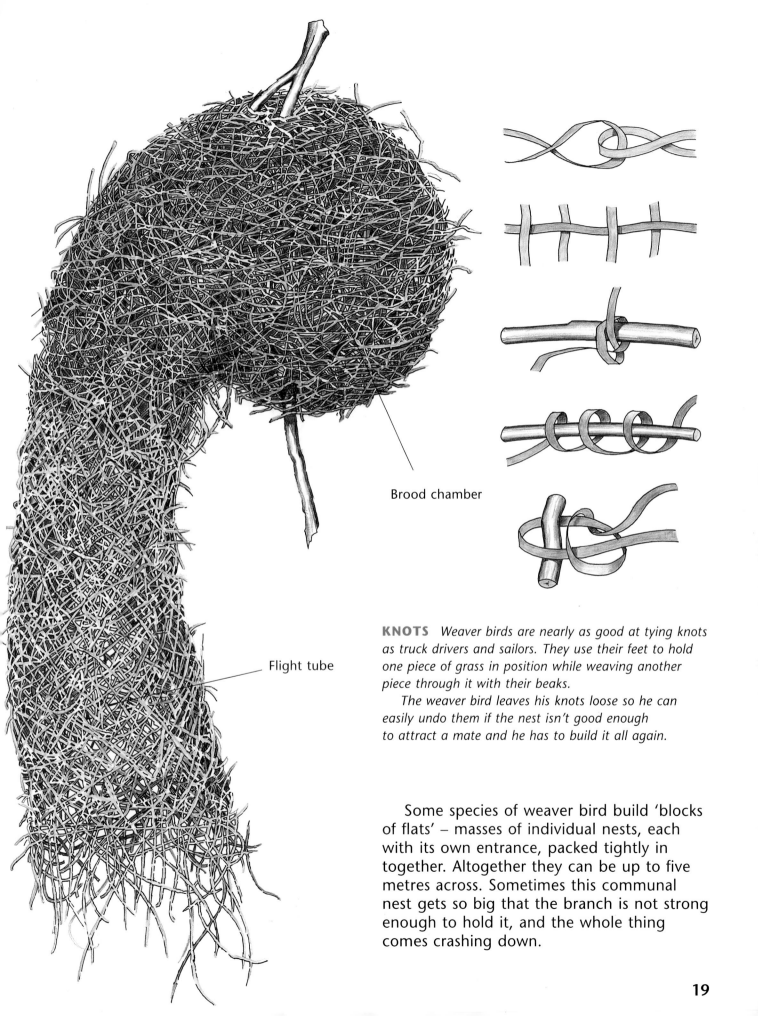

Brood chamber

Flight tube

KNOTS *Weaver birds are nearly as good at tying knots as truck drivers and sailors. They use their feet to hold one piece of grass in position while weaving another piece through it with their beaks.*

The weaver bird leaves his knots loose so he can easily undo them if the nest isn't good enough to attract a mate and he has to build it all again.

Some species of weaver bird build 'blocks of flats' – masses of individual nests, each with its own entrance, packed tightly in together. Altogether they can be up to five metres across. Sometimes this communal nest gets so big that the branch is not strong enough to hold it, and the whole thing comes crashing down.

Beautiful death traps
spiders' webs

Have you ever got up early on a cold morning and gone outside to look for a perfect spider's web, studded with hundreds of jewel-like droplets of dew? It's hard to believe that spiders create these beautiful objects just to capture and kill other creatures.

Spiders excrete long, very strong threads of silk from their bodies. They use these threads to make a variety of shapes – spirals, tubes, hammock shapes, cones and flat sheets. They coat the silk with a sticky substance to ensnare their prey.

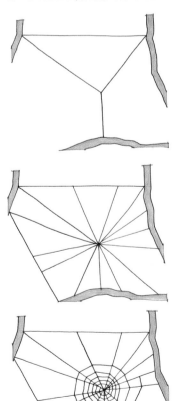

Constructing the web

Here's how a flat sheet is made.

1 The spider starts with a single long thread fixed at one end to a twig or branch as high up as possible. The spider allows the thread to float freely in the breeze until the other end sticks onto something else.

2 Using this line for support, the spider spins a second, looser thread.

3 Halfway along the second thread, it attaches a third thread hanging down. Pulling this tight, the spider attaches its bottom end to the ground or a lower branch.

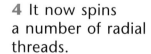

4 It now spins a number of radial threads.

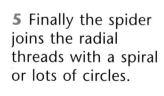

5 Finally the spider joins the radial threads with a spiral or lots of circles.

CHAPTER 4

CARPENTERS

Humans make wood into a building material by cutting it up into beams and boards. Most animals use it in a completely different way, hollowing out caves and tunnels in large pieces of wood. Only beavers actually cut trees down for their extensive engineering and architectural works.

Tree workshop
woodpecker

Woodpeckers have all the equipment needed by lumberjacks. Sharp claws and stiff tail-feathers allow them to perch securely on vertical tree-trunks while they peck at the wood and bark with their powerful beaks.

CUTAWAY DRAWING *showing that woodpeckers can carve nests even in the solid timber of living trees.*

They dig into trees, looking for insects and larvae to eat, and hollowing out nesting chambers.

Woodpeckers also use their beaks as drumsticks, beating on hollow branches to communicate with other birds.

Woodpeckers even have 'workshops'. They use a crevice in the bark or a crack in a piece of wood, as a vice to hold nuts or pinecones while they chip away at them. These 'workshops' are used over and over again, and the ground below becomes littered with wood chips, nut husks and broken pinecones.

Big construction projects *beaver*

Beavers change the natural environment more than any other animal, except humans.

They do this in order to create their own ideal habitat. Their engineering and construction works are carried out on a grand scale.

Once they have selected a good spot on a creek or river, they build a dam wall, to create a pond or small lake. Imagine having to build a dam before starting on your house!

In the middle of the pond they construct their lodge, a safe home with underwater entrances and a dry room inside. They chop down trees along the river banks to use as building materials. They even dig canals leading into the river so they can float logs to the dam site from further away.

One beaver family occupies each lodge. Young beavers leave home at two or three years old. When the parents die, one of the older offspring will start a new family and continue to occupy the pond. Some beaver dams are occupied and looked after for many generations. Beavers live for 10-15 years.

THE BEAVER, a construction specialist on land and under water
The beaver's large flat tail has several uses.
1 It acts as a rudder, when the beaver is swimming.
2 It can be used as a spare leg – a beaver holding a bundle of wood with its front legs can walk on its back legs, using its tail to balance.
3 It can be used as an alarm – beavers slap their tails hard on the water to warn each other of danger.

FOOD CACHE *Before winter comes and the pond freezes over, beavers make piles of food (leaves and bark) that they can swim to, under the ice, from the lodge.*

DAMS *Beavers use available materials – wood, rocks and mud – to create dams about a metre thick, up to 3 metres high, and as long as they need to be. The longest ever discovered was 700 metres! To strengthen the dam and stop the water washing* it away, they ram larger logs into the river bottom and brace them against big rocks or against trees on the river bank. The dam is not completely waterproof – water seeps slowly through it all the time.

Beavers have special valves and lids allowing them to seal up their nostrils, ears, eyes and mouth for underwater work.

Busy beavers

Beavers spend most of their lives cutting down trees. They strip off the leaves and bark to eat on the spot or store in underwater piles for later (winter) use. The trunks and branches are then used to build, improve or repair their dam and lodge. Beavers can cut down trees up to 1.2 metres thick and up to 50 metres away from the pond, dragging them along well-trodden paths or floating them along specially dug canals.

Beavers' large, strong front teeth are a bit like chisels – ideal for cutting down trees.

The front legs have 'fingers' for holding sticks and branches.

Webbed back feet make beavers strong swimmers.

LODGES Beavers build their lodge by piling up sticks and logs in the middle of the pool and weighing everything down with stones so it doesn't float away. Inside, above water level, they hollow out a dry living area, using chips of wood to make a soft, even floor. Two or more underwater entrances at the base of the lodge make it difficult for other animals to get in. The beavers smear the outside of the lodge with mud at the beginning of winter, which makes it waterproof.

Tunnels in wood *carpenter bee, woodworm*

Some animals feed their babies milk, some serve up bits of meat, some offer worms and grubs, and some whatever they can get their teeth into. For some animals, however, the preferred baby-food is wood. Many different kinds of beetles, flies, wasps, ants and moths lay their eggs in cracks and holes in pieces of wood. When the grubs hatch, they start eating the wood around them, creating a labyrinth of galleries and tunnels. Other parents dig the tunnels first, leaving plenty of 'sawdust' for the new arrivals to feed on.

Carpenter bees drill tunnels 30 cm long and 2.5 cm wide and then divide them into individual cells or rooms for their eggs, using wood chips to make the walls.

The most dramatic wood borer of all is not an insect, it's a mollusc (see page 6) called a 'shipworm', 'teredo', or 'marine borer'. It uses two tiny shells attached to its head to gnaw away at wooden ships, wharves or floating logs, creating long tunnels 2.5 cm wide – a snug home for its 1.5-metre worm-like body.

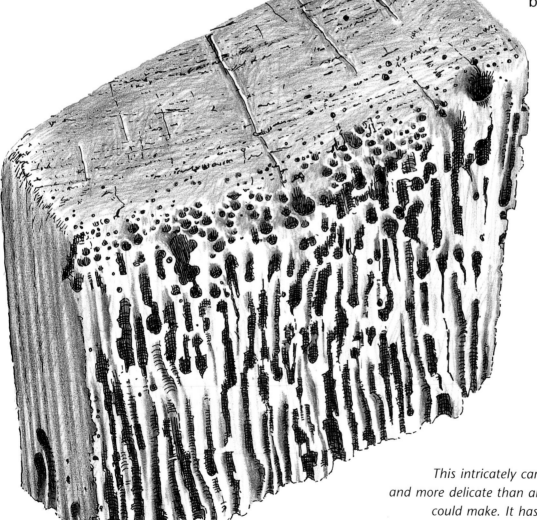

This intricately carved piece of wood is finer and more delicate than anything a human sculptor could make. It has been created by termites drilling a series of parallel tunnels along the grain of the timber, separated from each other by paper-thin walls of wood.

CHAPTER 5

BRICKLAYERS

Many animals use small lumps of mud or clay, piling them up to form walls, arches and domed roofs just as human bricklayers do. Certain birds are skilful mud-masons, but termites are the champions. Some termites build structures 8 metres tall. Remember that termites are only about 15 mm long, so their efforts are equivalent to humans building skyscrapers a kilometre high.

Double bubble
oven bird

This amazing little two-roomed clay bubble looks like a miniature baker's oven. It's not surprising that the builder is called an oven bird.

There are over 200 different species of oven bird in Central and South America. The male and female birds co-operate to bring about 2000 small lumps of mud to the building site, mixing in straw and animal dung to bind the mud together. A wall separates the 'entrance hall' from an inner breeding chamber. There is just enough room between the top of the wall and the domed roof for the birds to hop over. The breeding chamber is padded with fine grass.

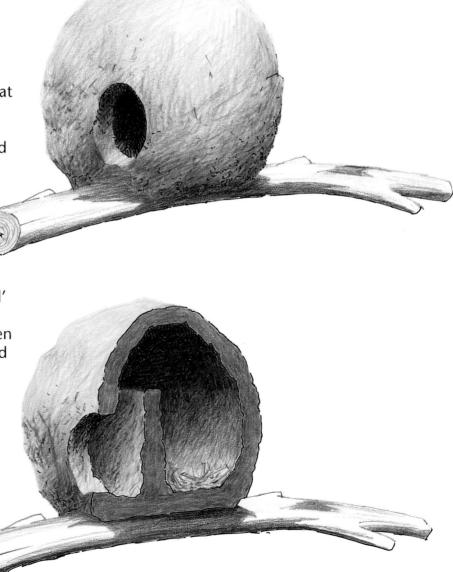

Skyscrapers of spit and sand *termite*

Huge 'vertical cities' house up to 2 000 000 termites. Some are as tall as a two-storey building. The external walls are a hard concrete-like material made of earth or sand combined with termite saliva. Internal walls are made of termites' saliva and faeces.

In the 'city of termites' each individual has its own job:
— **THE QUEEN** lies in a special chamber at the centre of the nest. She spends her life producing eggs from a huge, swollen abdomen. **THE KING** also lives in the royal chamber, mating with the queen so that she can produce eggs. **NYMPHS** are 'queens-in-waiting'. When the queen dies, one of this small group will take her place. **SOLDIERS** protect the nest, fighting off all intruders and guarding the workers as they go about their tasks. **WORKERS** Young workers carry eggs from the royal chamber to nearby 'nurseries', care for the larvae and young termites, build and repair the nest, feed and look after the king and queen. Older workers brave the outside world in search of food. They feed the soldiers and nymphs.

MOUND BUILT BY TERMITES IN THE KIMBERLEY REGION, NORTH-WEST AUSTRALIA

Some species of termites grow fungus in special rooms. The young larvae visit the fungus room to feed.

Royal chamber containing queen and king. He is much smaller than she is, but still bigger than the workers who feed them both and carry the new eggs away to 'nursery' chambers.

Eggs are carefully placed in 'nurseries' until they hatch.

The termites dig deep shafts – up to 40 metres long – in search of water to drink and use for building work.

'AIR-CONDITIONING' SYSTEM Two million termites in a nest of small tunnels and chambers would soon suffocate without a constant supply of fresh air. Some termite mounds have amazingly complicated ventilation systems.

A large empty cavern at the top of the mound fills up with stale, hot air that rises from the main part of the nest. The new hot air coming into this chamber pushes the air that has been there for a while into openings in the side walls.

The air in the side walls flows down tiny tunnels close to the outside of the mound. It cools down as it goes, exchanging poisonous carbon dioxide for life-giving oxygen, through the porous outer walls.

At the bottom, another large chamber stores the cool fresh air, which slowly rises up through the living areas of the nest. The termite nest sits right on top of this chamber, supported by a few columns.

In rainforest areas, Cubitermes *build a series of overhanging roofs to protect the walls of their nest from heavy rainfall.*

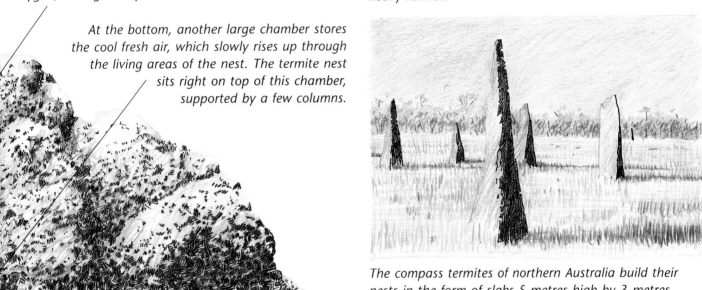

The compass termites of northern Australia build their nests in the form of slabs 5 metres high by 3 metres wide, running almost north-south. This orientation allows the sun to heat them up in the late afternoon (ready for the cold desert night) and again early in the morning. During the hot middle of the day the sun shines on the narrow edge of the slab, and not much heat is absorbed.

The living areas of the mound are swarming with termites, but the ventilation system is usually deserted, except when workers come to repair damaged areas.

Underground tunnels extend 3-4 metres out in all directions to entrances well away from the nest. Workers use these tunnels to go out at night in search of food. The termite mound itself does not have entrances.

A house of many chambers *bees, wasps*

The geometry of honeycomb

Honey bees build their nests inside hollow trees or in small caves. They hang vertical sheets of honeycomb side by side, leaving narrow spaces between. Each sheet of honeycomb is made up of two layers of hexagonal (six-sided) cells or chambers, back to back (their openings facing outwards). The bees construct the cells using wax excreted by special glands in their bodies.

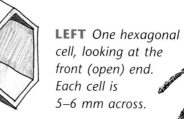

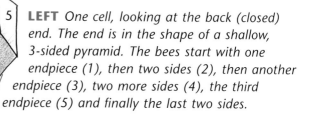

LEFT *One hexagonal cell, looking at the front (open) end. Each cell is 5–6 mm across.*

LEFT *One cell, looking at the back (closed) end. The end is in the shape of a shallow, 3-sided pyramid. The bees start with one endpiece (1), then two sides (2), then another endpiece (3), two more sides (4), the third endpiece (5) and finally the last two sides.*

FAR LEFT *Four cells together. Each cell fits snugly into its neighbours, sharing walls. The ends form a series of triangular 'hills' and triangular 'valleys' between the hills.*

LEFT *the second layer is arranged so that the end of each cell plugs into a 'valley' in the first layer. Again, the end pieces are shared.*

BELOW *While the sheets of honeycomb hang vertically, the cells actually tilt up a bit so that the honey won't pour out the ends.*

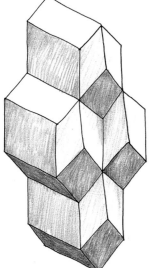

First the bees clump together in a tight ball. Their combined body heat is warm enough to soften the wax so that they can shape it. They start at the top, working their way down, hanging more and more cells onto the bottom. They leave a gap around the edge of the honeycomb so they can get from one sheet to another.

Some of the cells are used to store pollen and honey. Others have eggs (laid by the queen bee) placed in them – one in each cell – together with enough honey to feed the pupa (young bee) when it hatches.

Potter wasps

Potter wasps are 'solitary' wasps – they don't live in swarms as bees and some other wasps do. They are called 'potter wasps' because they build delicate little pots or jars out of clay. The female collects the clay, mixes it with water and presses it into long, thin strips. She places it in circular layers, building up a dainty little jar with a narrow neck. She fills it with food and then lays an egg in it. She closes the jar with a small piece of clay.

Some people say that the shape of these jars inspired early native American potters.

The female wasp provides a supply of paralysed grubs or caterpillars for the wasp larva to feed on when it hatches. When there is enough food in the 'jar', she lays an egg directly into it, hanging it from the top of the jar with a thread of mucus.

Mason wasps

Another solitary wasp, the mason wasp, chooses a flat surface and begins by building a series of arches out of mud or clay. The arches combine to form a short tunnel. The female wasp inserts an egg and a paralysed grub into the tunnel and then builds a wall to seal it off before extending the tunnel and repeating the process.

Honeycomb in a bottle

Many wasps, like bees, live in communities or swarms, and construct sheets of honeycomb to store food and eggs. In tropical regions of North and South America, *Polybia* wasps protect their honeycombs with a tough outer container that looks a bit like a big round bottle. The layers of honeycomb are fixed to the walls, leaving some gaps to allow the wasps to get from one layer to another. The nests hang in trees. They are about the size of a tennis ball. The outer walls are strong enough to protect the nest from the weather for many years.

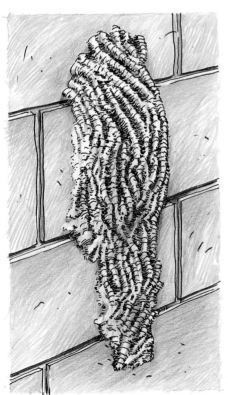

MASON WASP TUNNELS *on a brick wall*

The mason wasp's tunnels are divided into separate chambers, each containing an egg and a supply of food.

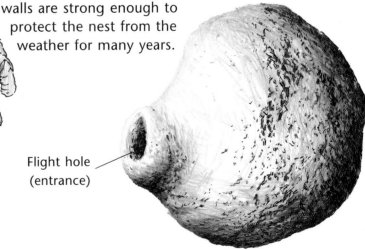

Flight hole (entrance)

The outer wall is made from a mixture of clay and sand. Inside, the hexagonal cells of the honeycomb are made of pure, fine clay. Unlike bee combs, they lie flat (horizontal), with the cells opening downwards. Wax lids stop the honey from pouring out.

Homes built to last: albatross and mudlark

Of all the great builders of the animal world, birds are the most versatile. They are champion weavers, woodworkers, diggers and mud-masons. I have chosen two birds' nests, both built of mud, to finish this book.

The shy albatross, an enormous bird with a 2.5-metre wingspan, builds this heavy platform of mud with a shallow bowl-shaped depression. It mixes its own faeces with the mud and works in a few straws and feathers to bind the whole thing together. The female lays her single egg in the middle. Once the egg has hatched, the adults go fishing, leaving the chick to maintain and repair the nest while they are away.

An albatross nest can be 50 cm across and 15 cm deep

This bird can be found almost anywhere in Australia, and it has a long list of names to go with its broad habitat. The magpie-lark, mudlark, Murray magpie, peewee or peewit builds a solid mud nest with vertical sides. The male and female birds work together. They select a good spot on a horizontal branch, then mix and carry the mud to build a nest with thick, high walls. Mudlarks sometimes build their nest on some other narrow horizontal object: part of a windmill, perhaps, or the framework of an open shed.

Glossary

abdomen back part of an insect
bolt-hole secret refuge or hideout
bower 'room' made of sticks and foliage
burrow hole(s) or tunnel(s) that an animal digs to live in
camouflage protective disguise or colouring that merges in with the background
carapace hard upper shell of a turtle, tortoise or crustacean
carbon dioxide colourless, odourless gas in the air. Animals produce carbon dioxide when they breathe
carnivorous meat-eating
crustacean a kind of invertebrate, usually completely covered by a hard shell, usually living in water
environment surrounding land, air, water, plants and animals
faeces solid animal or human waste; manure, dung, poo
habitat the type of natural environment in which an animal lives
hexagonal six-sided
instinct ability that animals are born with; a way of behaving that isn't taught
intertidal zone area of seashore between high and low tide
invertebrate animal with no backbone

keratin the material that hair, feathers, hooves, claws, horns and fingernails are made of
larva young insect at the stage between egg and pupa
lodge a beaver's home
mollusc soft-bodied invertebrate, usually having a hard shell
mucus slimy substance excreted by animals
nomad wanderer, person or animal that does not live in one place but keeps moving around
oxygen colourless, odourless gas essential for animals to breathe
plastron hard lower shell of a turtle, tortoise or crustacean
prairie treeless, grassy plains in North America
predator animal that naturally preys on and eats other animals
saliva spit
species particular kind of animal or plant. Members of one species can breed with each other, but not with members of another species
subterranean underground
ventilation movement of air within a building, or a means of getting rid of stale air and bringing fresh air in from outside
vice a tool used to hold something tight while you are working on it

Books consulted

A. Anderson and P. Jacklyn, *Termites of the Top End*, CSIRO Melbourne, 1993.
Australian Museum, *The Complete Book of Australian Mammals* (ed. Strahan), Collins/Angus & Robertson, Sydney, 1991.
J. Bletchley, *Insect and Marine Borer Damage to Timber and Woodwork*, London, 1967.
N. Dennis and D. Macdonald, *Meerkats*, New Holland, 1999.
A. Forsyth, *Mammals of North America*, Firefly, Buffalo NJ, 1999.
Frith, *Incubator Bird*, Scientific American, 1959.
The Grzimek Encyclopedia of Mammals, McGraw-Hill, New York, 1990.
Mitchell Beazley *Family Encyclopedia of Nature*, Mitchell Beazley International, London, 1992.
M. Saul, *Shells: An Illustrated Guide*, Doubleday, New York, 1974.
Simpson and Day, *Field Guide to the Birds of Australia*, 5th edn, Viking, Melbourne, 1996.
K. Von Frisch, *Animal Architecture*, Hutchinson, London, 1974.
E. Walker, *Mammals of the World*, 4th edn, Johns Hopkins University Press, Baltimore, 1983.
J. Woodford, *The Secret Life of Wombats*, Text, Melbourne, 2001.

Index

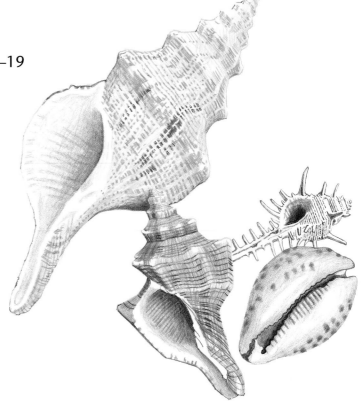